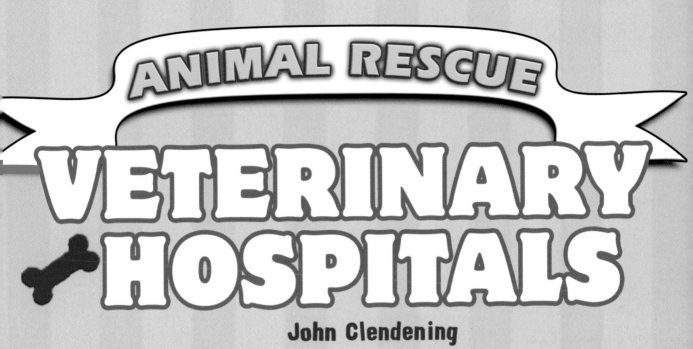

ANIMAL RESCUE

VETERINARY HOSPITALS

John Clendening

PowerKiDS
press

New York

Published in 2015 by The Rosen Publishing Group, Inc.
29 East 21st Street, New York, NY 10010

First Edition

Produced for Rosen by Cyan Candy, LLC
Editor: Joshua Shadowens
Designer: Erica Clendening, Cyan Candy

Photo Credits: All images Shutterstock.com

Library of Congress Cataloging-in-Publication Data

Clendening, John, author.
 Veterinary hospitals / by John Clendening. — 1st ed.
    pages cm. — (Animal rescue)
 Includes index.
 ISBN 978-1-4777-7023-8 (library binding) — ISBN 978-1-4777-7024-5 (pbk.) —
 ISBN 978-1-4777-7025-2 (6-pack)
 1. Veterinary hospitals—Juvenile literature. 2. Veterinary medicine—Juvenile literature. 3. Veterinarians—Juvenile literature. I. Title.
 SF604.55.C54 2015
 636.08'321—dc23
                                   2014003024

Manufactured in the United States of America

CPSIA Compliance Information: Batch #WS14PK8: For Further Information contact Rosen Publishing, New York, New York at 1-800-237-9932

TABLE OF CONTENTS

VETERINARY HOSPITALS

Veterinary hospitals are medical centers for the care of animals. They can be found in most communities since animals everywhere need medical care. **Veterinarians** are doctors trained to treat animals. Unlike doctors who provide care only to people, veterinarians must learn about many different types of animals.

There are many **biological** and **anatomical** differences among the various animals on Earth. This means that different types of animal bodies work differently from one another. Different animals also have different body structures. Veterinarians need to understand these differences so they can treat each animal correctly.

Animal Rescue!

Just as people's bodies are different from the bodies of other animals, the bodies of various animals are also different from one another. For example, a typical person has 206 bones in his body. A typical dog has 320 bones, and a typical cat has 230!

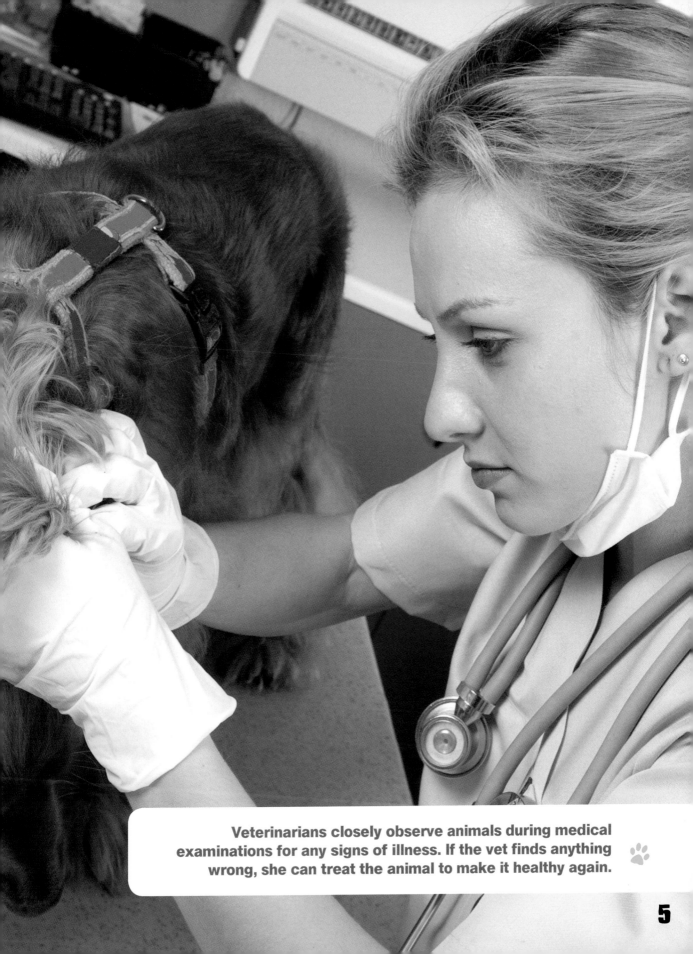

Veterinarians closely observe animals during medical examinations for any signs of illness. If the vet finds anything wrong, she can treat the animal to make it healthy again.

An important difference between veterinarians and other doctors is that veterinarians mainly rely on **clinical** signs of illnesses and injuries in animals. This is because animals cannot speak to tell veterinarians what is hurting them or how an injury happened. Veterinarians gather this clinical information by looking at, listening to, and touching animals to discover things that are **abnormal**, or not normal.

Veterinary hospitals are full of special medical equipment that veterinarians use to help sick or injured

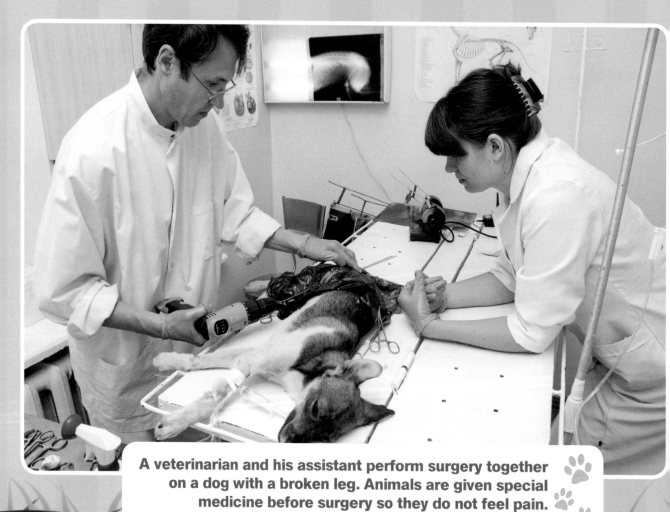

A veterinarian and his assistant perform surgery together on a dog with a broken leg. Animals are given special medicine before surgery so they do not feel pain.

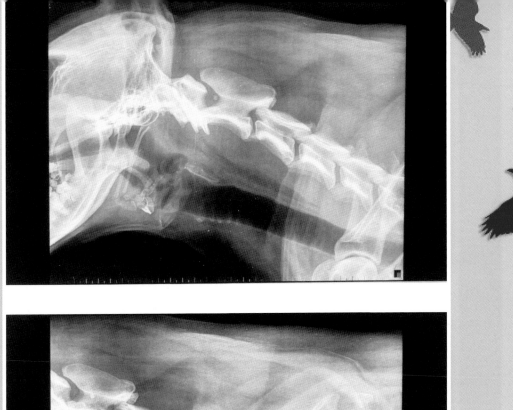

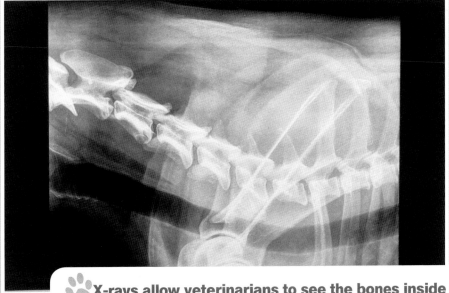

X-rays allow veterinarians to see the bones inside an animal. Special training is needed to be able to look at x-ray images to find broken bones or other problems.

animals. Much of the equipment is similar to what can be found in hospitals for people, like x-ray machines, so veterinarians can look inside animals for broken bones. They also have laboratory equipment so blood samples can be analyzed, as well as operating tables so that animal surgeries can be performed when necessary.

TYPES OF VETERINARY HOSPITALS

Veterinary hospitals vary in size and equipment and staff depending on what kinds of animals they treat and where they are located. In big cities, most animals that need medical care are small **companion animals**, or pets. The veterinary hospitals in these cities treat a lot of animals but are usually equipped only to treat smaller animals, such as dogs and cats.

There are an estimated 1.1 million cats and dogs living with people in New York City. With so many animals, New York City needs many veterinary hospitals.

In rural areas where people keep horses and raise large herds of cattle, some veterinary hospitals have a wider range of equipment. This range includes bigger equipment, so that the vets can treat animals both large and small.

Animal Rescue!

Veterinary hospitals can be very large, like the ones found in some big zoos. These kinds of hospitals need to be equipped to treat the many different types of animals that live there.

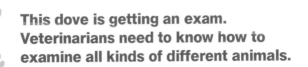

This dove is getting an exam. Veterinarians need to know how to examine all kinds of different animals.

Small veterinary hospitals serving a limited number of animal **species**, such as cats and dogs, are the most common. Most communities have at least one. These hospitals are usually owned and operated by veterinarians who work for themselves in **private practice**.

Most communities also have public veterinary hospitals operated by the animal control agencies of local governments. The veterinarians who work in these hospitals are employees of the city, county, or state in which they are located.

The number and size of both kinds of hospitals in a community is determined by local animal populations. Big cities with large animal populations usually have bigger public hospitals than smaller communities do. Big cities also usually have more small private hospitals since there are so many animals to serve.

Some animals get scared when they visit a veterinarian so it is helpful to have an assistant help the doctor handle animals. This Australian shepherd looks relaxed during its exam.

THE PEOPLE WHO WORK IN VETERINARY HOSPITALS

In veterinary hospitals, the highest level of medical care that animals receive comes from veterinarians. Doctors for people have nurses to assist them, and so do veterinarians. Veterinary nurses and technicians assist veterinarians with **routine**, or basic, tasks like weighing animals and giving shots.

As veterinarians do, nurses and technicians go to school to receive formal medical training in the care of animals. The difference among them is in the level of

This hose pumps gas that makes animals go to sleep when they breathe it. Animals need to be asleep for surgery so they do not move or feel pain.

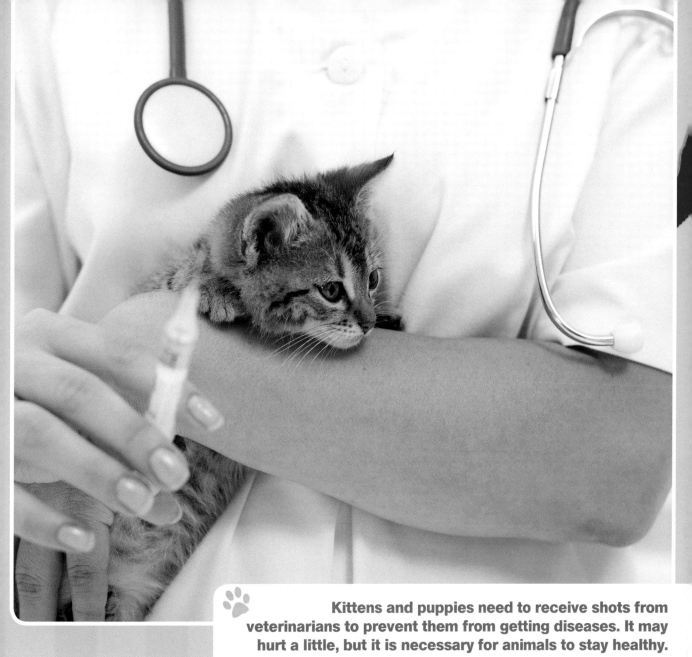

Kittens and puppies need to receive shots from veterinarians to prevent them from getting diseases. It may hurt a little, but it is necessary for animals to stay healthy.

education they achieve. All of them must take **specialized** animal science classes, but veterinarians go to school for more years than their assistants do. Some people who work in veterinarian hospitals do not need formal training in animal medicine but still perform important and necessary tasks. For example, receptionists answer phones, order supplies, and schedule appointments.

Veterinarians and their assistants can be trained in different areas of specialization. Some specialized areas of animal medicine are **exotic** animals, such as reptiles, small mammals, such as rabbits and ferrets, and birds. Another specialization is **equine** medicine, which is the medical care of horses.

Veterinarians can also further specialize by becoming experts not only on a specific animal species, but in the care of a specific animal body part. Some veterinarians become animal dentists and treat only animal teeth. Others become specialists in treating animal hearts, or even skin. Some veterinarians choose to specialize in performing surgeries.

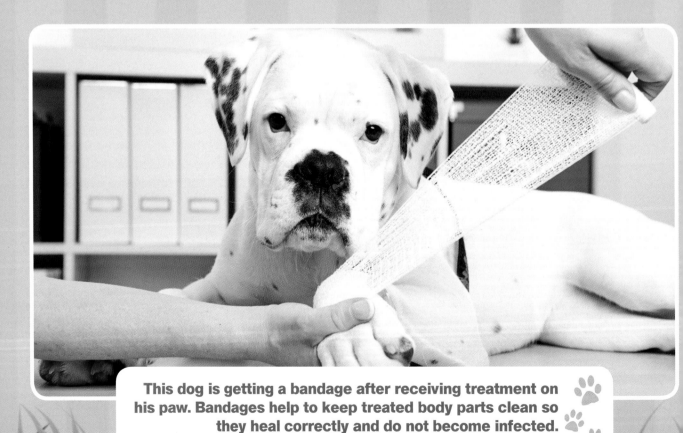

This dog is getting a bandage after receiving treatment on his paw. Bandages help to keep treated body parts clean so they heal correctly and do not become infected.

Cats go to the dentist too! Having clean teeth is important for overall health in both people and animals. Most cats need to be sleeping for veterinarians to clean their teeth.

Animal Rescue!

Wildlife medicine is a growing specialty area of veterinary medicine. Experts on wildlife are called out following oil spills or natural disasters to provide medical care to animals. For example, it is difficult to transport animals that live in the ocean, such as whales and dolphins, to veterinary hospitals.

HISTORY OF VETERINARY HOSPITALS

Our ancestors practiced animal medicine, but they did not have veterinary hospitals like we do today. Some of the oldest writings about animal medicine come from ancient texts from India, dating as far back as about 2,350 BC. Horses and elephants were useful in ancient India. They were used during wars to help people travel long distances and to carry the heavy loads of food, water, and gear that soldiers needed when far away from home.

The people of India have also always believed in the idea that all living beings are related. Because of this belief, most doctors in ancient India were trained to treat both humans and animals.

Veterinarians look and listen for many different things to examine the health of animals. Here a veterinarian is listening to a dog's heartbeat with a special instrument called a stethoscope.

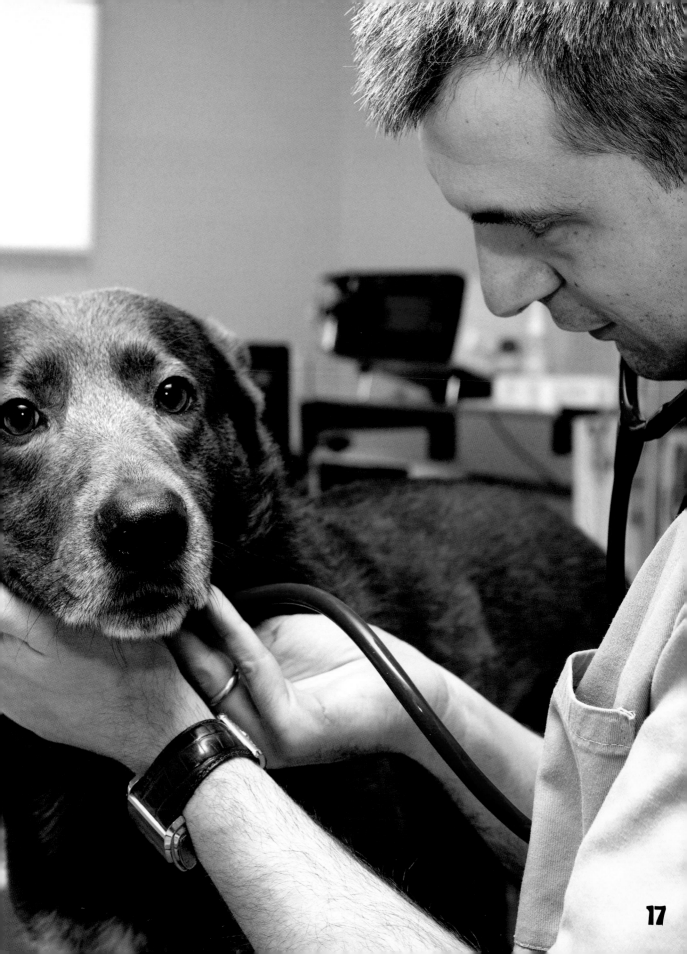

Horses have long been useful to people all over the world. **Farriers** are specialists in the care of horse **hooves**. To keep horses healthy to do work for us, farriers fit them with horseshoes to keep their feet from getting hurt. It takes special skills and knowledge to put shoes on a horse properly.

Over time, farriers became more knowledgeable about horse health in general and learned to treat more than just their hooves. Farriers in Europe shared their knowledge

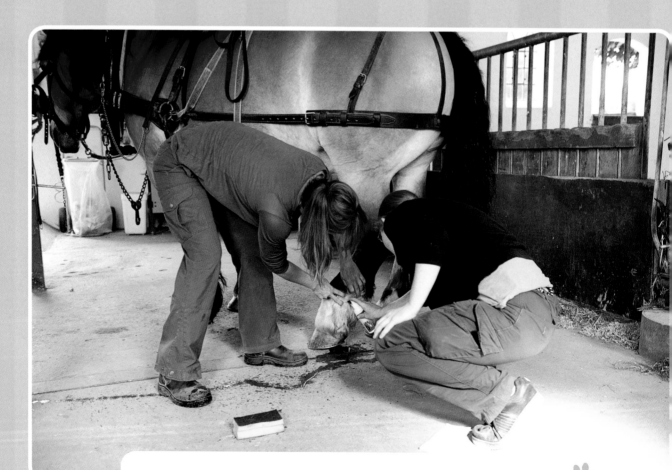

These women are cleaning a horse's hooves. Before horseshoes can be put on a horse, farriers must also trim the horse's nails to make sure the shoes fit comfortably.

Armies around the world still use horses today. This veterinarian with the United States Army inspects a horse's teeth during a routine medical examination to look for signs of illness.

Animal Rescue!

The world's very first veterinary college was founded in France in 1762. Other schools soon began to open in cities all over Europe. With formal professional training in animal medicine, and a growing number of professional veterinarians graduating from these schools, the creation of the first veterinary hospitals soon followed.

with each other and started professional groups as early as AD 475. These groups led to the formation of schools to train new farriers, and ultimately to the creation of the first veterinary hospitals.

VETERINARY HOSPITALS OF TODAY AND THE FUTURE

As animal medicine continues to evolve, veterinary hospitals also evolve and use the latest medical equipment and treatment methods. Hospitals also work towards improving their designs to offer more services and to feel more welcoming to animals.

In the past, many animal hospitals shared a similar and basic design. They had a small waiting room, with the examination rooms hidden from view in the back. The sights, sounds, and smells of many animals all waiting together in a small room made many of the animals afraid and uncomfortable to be there.

Animals should be calm and relaxed, not nervous and excited, when being examined. Veterinarians are trained to be very gentle with animals so their normal heart rates can be noted.

Veterinary hospitals try to make their waiting rooms as comfortable as possible for all of the people and animals waiting for their turns to see the veterinarian.

Animal Rescue!

Today, many new veterinary hospitals are bright, nicely decorated, and designed to make animals feel comfortable. These modern hospitals are often larger than they were in the past, and are staffed by friendly employees who comfort pets when they arrive, making them feel welcome.

Some modern medical equipment that veterinary hospitals use has been adapted from advances made in human medicine. The laparoscope is a camera on the end of a long tube that is inserted painlessly inside of an animal. Veterinarians today also increasingly use magnetic resonance imaging and ultrasound machines to see inside of animals.

All of these new technologies can help veterinarians identify health issues faster, allowing animals to be treated sooner. This can prevent other health problems that may arise from unnecessary surgeries.

Veterinary hospitals today also offer more services than ever in addition to animal medical care. It is becoming more and more common for them to offer things like animal behavior and training classes, pet ownership education classes, grooming services, dental services, and pet diet and nutrition programs.

Cats and dogs sometimes get their claws trimmed by veterinarians. People can also do this at home for their pets if they can get them to sit still long enough!

HOW TO BECOME A VETERINARIAN

If you love animals and have a strong desire to work with and help them, you may want to become a veterinarian. In America, veterinarians must complete college-level schooling and earn a degree in veterinary science or veterinary medicine. Veterinary students must then pass a national test to earn a **license** to be allowed to practice veterinary medicine.

Students get a lot of hands-on experience with animals while studying veterinary medicine in college. They also spend a lot of time in the classroom learning about animals.

Because many animals like cats and dogs have fur covering their entire bodies, the fur must be shaved off before veterinarians can cut into their skin for surgeries.

There are only 28 veterinary schools in America today that prepare students to take the licensing test after graduation. Because there are so few veterinary colleges, there is a lot of **competition** to get into these schools. Students who want to attend these schools must prepare long in advance and have excellent grades to be accepted.

People wanting to become veterinarians should also plan to have at least a few years of experience working with animals before applying to veterinary college. Good grades alone are not enough because of the heavy competition to get into veterinary colleges.

These schools want to see that applicants have experience working directly with animals. One of the best ways to gain this experience is by working alongside a veterinarian as a veterinary nurse, veterinary technician, or veterinary assistant.

Another great way to gain experience is to volunteer at an animal shelter. Virtually all animal shelters have a need for volunteers.

People and pets love and trust each other when they live together. Sometimes it is helpful for people to be with animals during veterinarian visits to help animals stay calm.

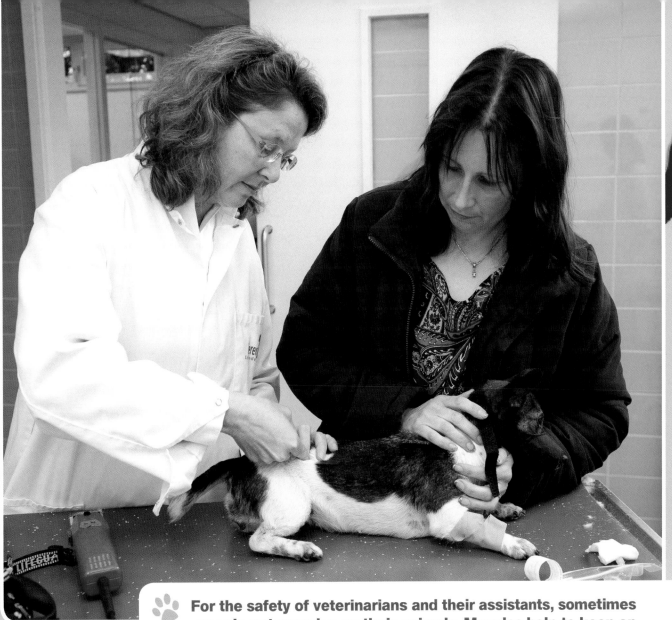

For the safety of veterinarians and their assistants, sometimes people put muzzles on their animals. Muzzles help to keep an animal's mouth closed temporarily so they cannot bite anyone.

Animal Rescue!

Minimum age requirements for volunteers in animal shelters vary from one shelter to another but are typically between 13 and 18 years old. People wanting to become veterinarians should start volunteering as early as possible to gain the years of experience working with animals that veterinary colleges look for in applicants.

FINAL THOUGHTS

Whether big or small, public or private, located in a city or the countryside, all veterinary hospitals strive to provide the best care possible to the animals they serve. There are millions of different species of animals on Earth, and each has specific health needs. Knowledge in the fields of animal medicine and animal science grows each year as veterinarians and their assistants continue to learn as much as they can about animals. New medical advances, and even new species of animals, are discovered regularly.

Human beings have kept animals as pets since before recorded history. And people also share the Earth with wild animals. Humans are unique in having the ability to study other animals and learn how to use medicine to help them when they need it.

A career as a veterinarian, veterinary nurse, or veterinary assistant can be very rewarding for people who love animals and want to help them be healthy and happy.

Humans and animals are unable to communicate with one another with words, yet we share our world, and some of us even share our homes. Humans have taken on the responsibility of helping sick and injured animals wherever and whenever we can. Veterinarians take this responsibility very seriously.

Veterinary hospitals provide communities with places in which sick, injured, and rescued animals can receive quality medical care when they need it. Veterinarians have saved countless animal lives in veterinary hospitals, and they continue to help and save more animals every day.

Animal Rescue!

In 2010, there was a large spill of almost 4 million gallons of oil into the Gulf of Mexico, which is home to many different kinds of marine animals. Veterinarians and marine animal experts were called to the scene to help animals injured by the oil spill.

GLOSSARY

abnormal (ab-NOR-mul) Out of the ordinary.

anatomical (uh-NAH-tah-mih-kul) Relating to the structure of an organism.

biological (by-uh-LAH-jih-kul) Related through birth.

clinical (KLIH-ni-kul) Involving direct observation of a patient.

companion animals (kum-PAN-yun A-nuh-mulz) Animals kept mainly for company or protection.

competition (kom-pih-TIH-shun) A game or test.

equine (EE-kwyn) An animal in the horse family.

exotic (ek-ZAH-tik) Strange or unusual.

farriers (FER-ee-erz) People who puts shoes on horses.

hooves (HOOVZ) The hard coverings on the feet of certain animals.

license (LY-suns) Official permission to do something.

private practice (PRY-vit PRAK-tes) The work of a doctor or lawyer who is self-employed.

routine (roo-TEEN) When someone does something the same way over and over.

specialized (SPEH-shuh-lyzd) To do something very well.

species (SPEE-sheez) A single kind of living thing. All people are one species.

veterinarians (veh-tuh-ruh-NER-ee-unz) Doctors who treat animals.

INDEX

WEBSITES

Due to the changing nature of Internet links, PowerKids Press has developed an online list of websites related to the subject of this book. This site is updated regularly. Please use this link to access the list: **www.powerkids.com/ares/hosp/**